A Victorian Childhood

At Play

Ruth Thomson

FRANKLIN WATTS
LONDON • SYDNEY

First published in 2007 by Franklin Watts
338 Euston Road, London NW1 3BH

Franklin Watts Australia
Level 17/207 Kent Street
Sydney NSW 2000

Designer: Mei Lim
Editor: Susie Brooks

The author would like to thank John and Sandy Howarth
of Swiss Cottage Antiques, Leeds and Islington Education
Library Service (www.objectlessons.org) for the loan of
items from their collection, and Bella Bennett.

Photographic acknowledgements
Neil Thomson 2/3, 5, 6, 7, 8br, 9c, 9bl, 10t, 11, 13, 16t, 17,
20l, 24c, 26, 27; Peter Millard/Franklin Watts Picture
Library 10b, 24t; London Metropolitan Archives: 22c;
NTPL/Andreas von Einsiedel 4c.

A CIP catalogue record for this book is available
from the British Library.

Dewey Classification: 790.9

ISBN 978 0 7496 7052 8

Printed and bound in Malaysia

Franklin Watts is a division of Hachette Children's Books.

Contents

THE NURSERY

Rich and poor Victorian children led very different lives. Many poor children had to work. They had little time for play and no money for books and toys. Well-off children led a more sheltered life at home and had plenty of time for play.

A room full of toys

Children in well-off families had a room, called the nursery, at the top of the house. This was both their schoolroom and their playroom. It was full of toys, games and books.

This is the reconstructed Victorian nursery in a grand house, called Lanhydrock, in Cornwall.

Toys for all tastes

Boys and girls were given different toys.
Girls played with dolls, dolls' houses and
miniature household equipment. Boys played
with toy soldiers, trains or did science experiments.

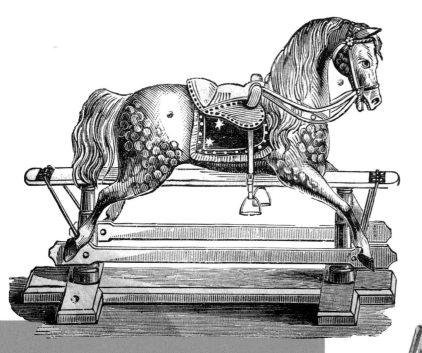

▲ Toy soldiers

Rocking horses were the pride of the
nursery. They were realistically carved
and hand-painted, with pricked ears
and a long neck. The finest ones had
real horsehair manes and tails.

Books of all kinds

Until the middle of Queen Victoria's reign, most
children's books were educational or told
stern **moral** tales, such as *Struwwelpeter*.
By the end of the 19th century, many
more books were being written purely
for children's amusement, such as
Treasure Island, *The Jungle Book* and *Alice in
Wonderland*. There were also illustrated nursery
rhyme and picture books for younger children.

▲ Books and magazines
of the late 1800s

INDOOR PLAY

Well-off Victorian children amused themselves with board games, dressing up and performing plays, playing word games and learning tricks.

Table games

Children played traditional games, such as draughts, dominoes and solitaire, as well as new ones. The game of halma was invented in 1888. Players had to cross their playing pieces from one side of a board to the other. Tiddleywinks was another newly invented game. Players had to flip pieces from a table into a cup.

▲ Father and son playing halma

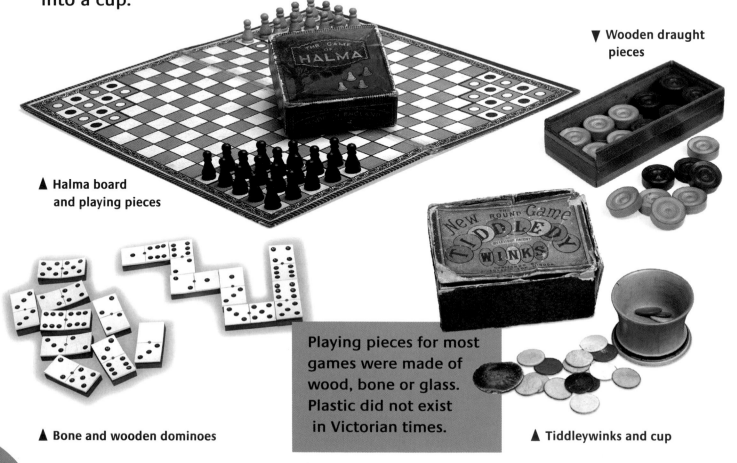

▼ Wooden draught pieces

▲ Halma board and playing pieces

Playing pieces for most games were made of wood, bone or glass. Plastic did not exist in Victorian times.

▲ Bone and wooden dominoes

▲ Tiddleywinks and cup

◀ Book of games

Party games

At parties, children played games that are still played today, such as musical chairs, blind man's buff and Simon says. Charades was a very popular game, where people acted out words for other players to guess.

Tricks and puzzles

Many children were very keen on magic and scientific tricks, number puzzles, and word games such as guessing riddles, **anagrams** and **proverbs**. Children's magazines often included puzzle competitions.

Putting on plays

Some children and their friends enjoyed learning plays and performing them in front of their families. They dressed up and made their own props.

A puzzle from *A Book of Games*

SIX AND FIVE MAKE NINE
This is a simple little puzzle. Take eleven strips of cardboard, lay six of them at exactly equal distances on the table.

| | | | |

Ask one of the company to add five other strips and yet only make nine. It is done by placing them as in the dotted lines, thus:

▲ Script of a children's play

7

PASTIMES

Well-off families also entertained themselves at home with music, hobbies or shows.

Magic Lanterns

Victorians invented all sorts of amusements. Magic lantern shows were popular at children's parties and at Christmas. Hand-painted glass **slides** were moved in front of the light of a lantern and projected on to a screen.

The beam of light in a magic lantern came from a gas or oil lamp.

People marvelled at being able to hear music on a machine.

Sounds and pictures

The gramophone was the first machine to play recordings on flat disks called records. The zoetrope was a toy which seemed to make pictures move. A strip of sequenced pictures was put into a drum with slits. When viewers looked through the slits as the drum was spinning, they saw only one 'moving' image.

▲ **Replica** zoetrope and pictures

Making music

Wealthy and middle-class girls spent most of their day at home. Most households owned a piano and piano playing was considered an important **accomplishment** for girls. They played to entertain their family and guests.

◄ Piano practice

Needlework

Sewing was another skill that all girls were expected to learn. They spent a lot of time practising different stitches by making samplers, which included both letters and pictures.

▲ Sampler

Girls usually signed and dated their sampler and included their age, as well.

▲ Victorian scrapbook and scraps

Collections

Many children enjoyed cutting, arranging and pasting coloured scraps into a scrapbook. They bought the scraps in sheets, which had pictures joined by tabs. Others liked making collections of coins, stamps, postmarks, flowers or shells.

SUNDAYS

Sundays were seen by respectable Victorians as days of rest and prayer. Children were not allowed to play with their usual toys and games.

Quiet play

After going to church and **Sunday School**, children were expected to find quiet ways to amuse themselves during the long afternoon.

Children dressed in their best clothes on Sundays – girls often wore white dresses with frills and boys wore suits.

A Sunday toy

A Noah's Ark was one of the only toys children were allowed to play with on Sundays, because it depicted a Bible story. Children could re-enact Noah lining up animals in pairs to go into the Ark, to escape the coming Flood. Often, however, children made up their own stories about the animals.

This Ark and animals have been hand-carved from wood and painted in realistic, bright colours.

Sunday books

Some children's books and magazines were especially written to be read on Sundays. Many stories were religious; others were adventure or school tales with a moral. There were also poems to learn, competitions to enter and pages to colour. These books were often given to children as Sunday School prizes.

The cover of this Sunday book reminded children to give to others less fortunate than themselves.

▲ Religious colouring picture

Bible reading

At the end of Sunday, families often gathered in the front room and the father read aloud from the Bible.

An extract from *The Children's Treasury of Pictures and Stories*, 1899

A little girl asked her mother, "Which is worse – to tell a lie or to steal?"

The mother, taken by surprise replied that both were so bad she couldn't tell which was worse.

"Well," said the little girl, "I've been thinking that it is worse to lie than to steal. If you steal a thing, you can take it back or pay for it, but a lie is for ever!"

OUTDOOR FUN

Country children spent much of their time outside. Wealthier city children had gardens to play in, but those from poor families had little fresh air or exercise.

City spaces

▲ Drinking fountain

Industrial cities had become overcrowded and polluted, as more and more people came to them to work. People realised that these filthy surroundings were spreading disease, so they started widening streets and building public parks. The spacious parks meant that people could stroll in the fresh air. Many parks had drinking fountains, **bandstands** for musicians, a boating lake, benches and shelters.

Children play in a sandpit at this city park. Notice that all the boys are wearing caps and all the girls are wearing hats.

Country children

Most country children had to help with chores and farmwork and had little time for play. In their free time, they played with hoops, tops and marbles or roamed the fields, watching birds and wildlife.

Natural pleasures

Boys climbed trees in search of birds' nests, went fishing, followed animal tracks and made whistles and pop-guns from twigs. Girls collected flowers or played skipping and rhyming games.

The autumn was a time for picking nuts and blackberries, and for gathering mushrooms.

Cycling around

After bicycles were invented in the 1880s, cycling quickly became a popular sport. Roads, especially those in the country, were very safe and quiet for cyclists, because there were no cars.

PHILIPS' CYCLISTS' MAP OF THE COUNTY OF YORKSHIRE N.W. SHEWING THE MAIN ROADS DISTINCTLY COLOURED REDUCED FROM THE ORDNANCE SURVEY PRICE ONE SHILLING. GEORGE PHILIP & SON. 32, FLEET STREET, LONDON; AND LIVERPOOL.

Cycling map ▶

Older boys joined cycling clubs that organised rides into the country.

SPORTS

Team sports, such as football, rugby and cricket, were played in boys' **public schools**, such as Eton, Harrow and Rugby. These schools were the first to organise these games and lay down a set of rules.

Footballers wore long-sleeved shirts with collars, long shorts and leather ankle boots.

Football

Children played football in the street or in fields, using a blown-up pig's bladder as a ball. The game was rough and rules varied. In 1863, some men got together and formed the Football Association. They agreed on definite rules. Some footballers became professionals – paid to play for a club. By the end of the century, watching football matches had become a popular activity.

From the 1870s onwards, factories made leather footballs of a standard size and weight.

Cricket

In early Victorian times, cricket was part of country life. It was played on village greens with a curved bat. The ball was bowled underarm and there were no real rules until 1835. Cricket became very popular among well-to-do boys at public schools, who continued playing once they grew up and formed cricket clubs.

A game of cricket ▼

Badminton

The modern sport of badminton started in 1893, when an Association agreed a set of rules. It grew out of a popular children's game, called battledore and shuttlecock. Two players hit a shuttlecock (a small, feathered cork) to and fro with bats called battledores. They tried to keep the shuttlecock in the air for as many hits as possible.

Unlike badminton, battledore and shuttlecock did not need a net or a court. It was played in the street.

15

STREET GAMES

Children from poor families had very few toys and lived in small, overcrowded homes with no space to play indoors. Instead, they played games in the street.

▼ Hopscotch

Skipping ▼

A skipping rhyme
All in. A bottle of gin.
All out. A bottle of stout.
All in together.
Frosty weather.

Fun for free

Children used what they could find for their games. They skipped with a length of old rope. They scratched a hopscotch court in the ground. They hung a rope around a lamp-post as a swing. They played a game called five-stones, where they threw five pebbles into the air and tried to catch as many as possible on the back of one hand. They also played tag and leap-frog.

▲ Leap-frog

Marbles

Boys liked playing with marbles. The cheapest ones were made from clay; others were made from stone or coloured glass. Lemonade bottles had clear glass marbles as stoppers. Children broke the bottles to get the marbles out.

▼ Lemonade bottle

Boys dug a hole in the ground and tried to throw a handful of ten marbles into the hole at once.

▲ Clay marbles

Whipping tops

A wooden whipping top was a cheap, popular toy to buy. A leather or string whip was wound around the cone-shaped top. Children put their top on the ground and quickly pulled away the whip. The child whose top kept spinning for the longest was the winner.

Spinning a top on your hand was a skill that needed lots of practice.

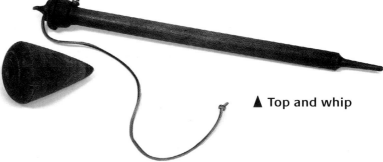

▲ Top and whip

ENTERTAINMENT

All sorts of entertainers performed in the streets. There were musicians and shows, and, occasionally, a bear, which stood on its hind legs to dance.

Seasonal shows

Children only went to the theatre at Christmas, to see a **pantomime** with their family as a special treat. Sometimes they went to the circus. There was great excitement when, once a year, a travelling fair came to town with its steam-driven rides.

Punch and Judy shows took place on street corners. A drummer banged loudly to attract an audience.

Men wandered through busy streets, wearing boards like these, to advertise a pantomime.

DRURY LANE THEATRE
THE
BABES
THE
OOD

Circus show ▲

Street music

In large towns and cities, musicians filled the streets and markets with their tunes, hoping people would give them a penny or two. There were Scottish bagpipe players, Italian violinists and harpists, and **barrel organ** grinders, who often trained a tame monkey to collect money.

Military brass bands played free concerts at bandstands in parks and at the seaside.

OUTINGS

Children from well-off families sometimes went to places of interest as a special treat.

Picnics

In the summer, families went on picnics. Mrs Beeton, in her book of household management, suggested a picnic menu for children of ham and beef sandwiches, cold meat rolls, fruit and jam puffs, cakes, fresh fruit, home-made lemonade, lime-juice cordials and water.

▲ Family picnic

An elephant ride was the exciting highlight of a visit to the zoo.

Educational visits

The Victorians were the first to build free public libraries, museums and zoos (known then as zoological gardens). Zoos gave children the chance to see live wild animals, such as bears, tigers, lions, monkeys and exotic birds. Natural history museums displayed stuffed animals, fossils, skeletons and rocks.

Sunday School outings

The only treat that the poorest children ever had was a yearly **Ragged School** or Sunday School outing to the nearest patch of countryside or a day trip to the sea.

These pictures were on the front page of a newspaper, illustrating an article about a country outing for Ragged School children.

▲ Children waiting for a tram-car

▲ Long swing for the girls

▲ Game of cricket for the boys

Extract from
The Daily Graphic, August 28, 1891

Three or four mornings in every week, a little crowd of more or less ragged children may be seen on the pathway in Mile End Road waiting for the special tram-cars that will take them to the borders at Epping Forest.

MARCHING INTO THE FOREST

Arrived at Walthamstow, the crowd of fully a hundred children is formed into a **procession** and they march onwards to the 'retreat'. Here in a canvas-roofed shed, decorated with illuminated texts, the long wooden tables are spread with cups and plates for breakfast. But before they begin, the director has a few words about the love of God, the evils of drink and of kindness to one another.

ROMPING ON THE GREEN

After breakfast there are two roundabouts and two long swings – one for boys and one for girls; cricket balls and stumps, hoops and toys of all sorts are distributed and play begins in earnest. They are a troublesome little crowd. "They won't let me play with them."; "This boy hit me."; "He's took my hoop." are frequent complaints.

Why do you think this outing was reported in a newspaper?
- What games were provided for the children?
- What else were they given?
- What did the director talk about to them? Why did he do this?

HOLIDAYS

The main holidays that people celebrated were Easter, May Day, **Whitsun** and Christmas.

May Day

On May Day (1st May), children in villages chose a girl to be the May Queen. They made a large garland of flowers and paraded with it, dressed in their best clothes. They stopped at houses to sing a song and ended the day with a huge tea. Another May Day custom was to dance around a maypole, holding brightly coloured ribbons.

Dancing around a maypole on May Day happened even in some city schools.

Children from each Sunday School marched behind their own banner.

Whitsun

Whitsun was a religious holiday, but it also marked the beginning of summer. Children were bought new clothes – girls got a straw hat with ribbons and boys got a new jersey or pair of trousers. Many children wore their new clothes to go on a Whitsun Walk with their Sunday School. All the Sunday Schools in a town joined together in a procession, with their embroidered **banners** flying.

Christmas time

Many Christmas traditions, such as sending cards, decorating the house and putting up a fir tree, carol singing, pulling crackers, eating turkey and Father Christmas, started in Victorian times.

Boxing Day

Boxing Day (26th December) got its name because this was the day when wealthy people gave boxes of gifts to their servants, and small sums of money to **tradesmen** who regularly called at their house.

▲ Victorian Christmas cards

What toys is Father Christmas carrying?
- Which of these toys might children receive now?
- How does the image of Father Christmas differ today?

THE SEASIDE

Only the well-off went to the seaside in early Victorian times. Poor families were not paid for time off work, so they could not afford holidays. After **Bank Holidays** began in 1871, workers took day trips to the seaside.

Weston-super-Mare

Resorts with railway lines grew rapidly as workers started to come by train on day trips.

On the beach

Holidaymakers sat on the beach and paddled in the sea, just as people do today. Everyone kept their clothes on and wore a hat. Women changed for swimming inside a hut on wheels called a bathing machine, which was pushed into the sea. There were entertainments and shellfish, lemonade and ice cream stalls.

How do these seaside activities from 1890 differ from those today?

▲ Sitting on deck chairs

▲ Drying clothes

▲ Bathing machine

▲ Punch and Judy show

▲ Paddling

▲ Barrel organ and monkey

▲ Donkey rides

Picture postcards started in 1894. They showed seaside scenes with a pier and promenade – the pride of every big resort.

Seaside attractions

Every resort had a seafront promenade, where people could stroll and show off their best clothes. Some also had a Winter Garden, a building with a glass roof, where people could eat and dance in bad weather. Other attractions were aquariums, gardens with bandstands, boating lakes and souvenir shops.

People could watch a show and have a meal in the pavilion at the end of the pier.

The pier

Big resorts had a long, cast-iron **pier**. People paid a few pence to enjoy a breezy walk over the sea and watch entertainers.

FINDING OUT MORE

See what you can find out about Victorian toys, games, outings and holidays for yourself.

Toys

Look at illustrations in Victorian children's books. Notice what toys children are playing with. Are any of the toys the same as yours?

Sports

Find out about the history of your favourite sport.

- When did it start?
- Where was it played?
- What equipment did the players use?
- What special clothes did the players wear?
- What were the rules?
- How did the rules change?

Books

Look in libraries or second-hand bookshops for books about Victorian games, puzzles, tricks and toys.

Parks

Are there any Victorian features in your local park, such as a bandstand, a water fountain or iron gates?

▲ Park entrance gates   ▲ Bandstand

Conundrums (riddles) from a Victorian book of puzzles called *Guess Me*

- Why is the letter K like a pig's tail? Because it's at the end of por*k*.
- If a tree were to break a window, what would the window say? *Tre–mendous.*
- When you put on your slippers, why do you always make a mistake? Because you *put your foot in it.*
- Why is a fishmonger never generous? Because his business makes him *selfish* (sell fish).
- When is a clock on the stairs dangerous? When it *runs down* and strikes *one.*
- What belongs to yourself, but is used more by your friends than by yourself? *Your name.*

Photographs

Look carefully at photographs of Victorian children.
They were often posed holding a toy.

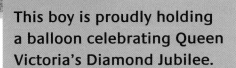

This boy is proudly holding
a balloon celebrating Queen
Victoria's Diamond Jubilee.

The seaside

Many features of seaside resorts were built
by the Victorians. Look out for some of these.

▲ Promenade

▲ Holiday house

▲ Cast-iron benches

▲ Fountain

▲ Pier

TIMELINE

1830s

1837 Queen Victoria came to the throne.

1840s

1843 The first Christmas card was sent.

1846 Prince Albert, Queen Victoria's husband, made the German custom of decorating a Christmas tree fashionable in England.

1847 London Zoo was opened to paying visitors.

1870s

1871 The Rugby Football Union was formed to set standard rules for Rugby Football.

1871 Bank Holidays started.

1872 The first FA Cup Final was played. Wanderers beat the Royal Engineers 1–0.

1872 The first Penny Farthing bicycle was introduced.

1873 Major Wingfield invented lawn tennis.

1877 The All England Croquet Club held the first Wimbledon Lawn Tennis championships – for men only.

1890s

1890 The first comic in England, called *Comic Cuts*, was published.

1891 Basketball was invented by James Naismith, a Canadian.

1894 *The Jungle Book* was written by Rudyard Kipling.

1894 Moving pictures were invented by the Lumière Brothers in France.

1850s

1850 The Public Libraries Act enabled towns to build free public libraries.

1853 The first modern cricket bat was made.

1853 The first public aquarium was opened at London Zoo.

1860s

1864 Overarm bowling in cricket was allowed for the first time.

1865 *Alice in Wonderland* was written by Lewis Carroll.

1880s

1883 *Treasure Island* by Robert Louis Stevenson was published.

1885 The 'safety' bicycle, with equal-sized wheels and a chain, was invented.

1887 Queen Victoria's Golden Jubilee (50 years on the throne) took place.

1887 The gramophone was invented by Emile Berliner.

1888 The Football League was founded by 12 football clubs.

1900s

1895 The wireless (radio) was invented by Guglielmo Marconi.

1897 Queen Victoria's Diamond Jubilee (60 years on the throne) took place.

1899 The Blackpool Tower, the landmark of the seaside resort of Blackpool, was opened.

1901 Queen Victoria died.

29

GLOSSARY

accomplishment something that someone is very good at

anagram a word or sentence with the same letters as another word or sentence but in a different order, for example **who** is an anagram of **how**

bandstand a structure that shelters a group of musicians

Bank Holiday one of several weekdays (often Mondays) in the year when banks, shops and factories are officially shut

banner a large piece of cloth with pictures or writing on it, attached to long poles that people can carry

barrel organ an organ that is played by turning a barrel inside it with a handle. Notches on the barrel play a particular tune

moral relating to character or behaviour considered good or bad

pantomime a show usually put on at Christmas time, often based on a fairy tale, that includes singing, dancing and funny characters and costumes

pier a long, high platform built out into the sea, which people can walk along to admire the view of the land and sea

procession a long line of people walking along, one behind the other

proverb a short sentence that gives advice or expresses a truth

public school a well-thought of boarding school for boys, which parents paid for

Ragged School a free Victorian school for the very poorest children

replica a new, exact model of something that was made before

resort a place where people go for their holidays

slide a small, transparent picture put into a magic lantern or projector to be shown on a screen

Sunday School a school attached to a church where children learned about Christian beliefs and the Bible

tradesmen shopkeepers or skilled workmen who called at houses

Whitsun a Christian festival, held fifty days after Easter

PLACES TO VISIT

Most of the museums below have exhibitions of toys, including Victorian ones. Some also have a reconstructed nursery.

Beaumaris Museum of Childhood Memories
1 Castle Street, Beaumaris LL58 8AP
www. beaumaris.org.uk/attractions.html

Bethnal Green Museum of Childhood
Cambridge Heath Road, London E2 9PA
www.vam.ac.uk/moc/index.html

Blaise Castle House Museum
Henbury Road, Bristol BS I0 7QS
www. bristol-link.co.uk/history/blaise-castle-museum.htm

Brighton Toy and Model Museum
52-55 Trafalgar Street, Brighton BN1 4EB
www.brightontoymuseum.co.uk

Cambridge and County Folk Museum
2/3 Castle Street, Cambridge CB3 0AQ
www.folkmuseum.org.uk

Cecil Higgins Art Gallery
Castle Lane, Bedford MK40 3RP
www.cecilhigginsartgallery.org

Dorking and District Museum
62 West Street, Dorking, Surrey RH4 1BS
www.dorkingmuseum.co.uk

Edinburgh Museum of Childhood
42 High Street, Royal Mile, Edinburgh EH1 1TG
www.cac.org.uk

The House on the Hill Toy Museum
Stansted Mountfitchet, Essex CM24 8SP
www.stanstedtoymuseum.com

Hove Museum and Art Gallery
19 New Church Road, Hove, East Sussex BN3 4AB
www.hove.virtualmuseum.info

Ilkley Toy Museum
Whitton Croft Road, Ilkley, West Yorkshire LS29 9HR
www.ilkleytoymuseum.co.uk

Isle of Skye Toy Museum
Holmisdale House, Glendale, Isle of Skye IV55 8WS
www.toy-museum.co.uk

Judges' Lodgings, Gillow Museum and Museum of Childhood
Church Street, Lancaster LA1 1YS
www.lancashire.gov.uk/education/museums/lancaster/judges.asp

Kirkstall Abbey House Museum
Abbey Road, Kirkstall, Leeds LS5 3EH
www.leeds.gov.uk/abbeyhouse

Lanhydrock
Bodmin, Cornwall PL30 5AD
www.nationaltrust.org.uk

Lilliput Mueum of Antique Dolls and Toys
High Street, Brading, Isle of Wight PO36 0DJ
www.lilliputshop.com

Royal Tunbridge Wells Museum
Civic Centre, Mount Pleasant, Tunbridge Wells, Kent TN1 1JN
www.tunbridgewellsmuseum.org

St Fagans National History Museum (Wales)
St Fagans, Cardiff CF5 6XB
www.museumwales.ac.uk/en/stfagans

Snowshill Manor
Near Broadway, Gloucestershire WR12 7JU
www.nationaltrust.org.uk

Sudbury Hall – The National Trust Museum of Childhood
Sudbury, Ashbourne, Derbyshire DE6 5HT
www.nationaltrust.org.uk

Worthing Museum and Art Gallery
Chapel Road, Worthing, West Sussex BN11 1HP
www.worthing.gov.uk/Leisure/MuseumampArtGallery

Yesterday's World
89–90 High Street, Battle, East Sussex TN33 0AQ
www.yesterdaysworld.co.uk

York Castle Museum
Eye of York, York YO1 9RY
www.yorkcastlemuseum.org.uk

INDEX

These are the lists of contents for each title in *A Victorian Childhood:*

At Home
The move to towns • Homes for poor people • Suburbs • Comfortable homes • Heat and light • Washing and baths • Families • Babies • Health and illness • Clothes • Keeping in touch

At Play
The nursery • Indoor play • Pastimes • Sundays • Outdoor fun • Sports • Street games • Entertainment • Outings • Holidays • The Seaside

At School
Early schools • Schools for all • The classroom • The school day • Learning to write • Other subjects • Boys' lessons • Girls' lessons • Exercise and hygiene • Absences • Punishments and rewards

At Work
Child workers • Nasty jobs • On the farm • In the home • Cottage industries • Shop boys • Street sellers • Guttersnipes • Scavengers • Helping children • Schools